First Field Guide
to Australian
MAMMALS

Written by Pat Slater
Photography by Steve Parish

PASCAL PRESS

Contents

Australia's mammals	4
How to see mammals	5
What mammal is it?	6
Naming mammals	7
Spot the mammal	8

Mammals

Platypus	10
Short-beaked Echidna	11
Brush-tailed Phascogale	12
Yellow-footed Antechinus	13
Fat-tailed Dunnart	14
Kultarr	15
Spotted-tailed Quoll	16
Tasmanian Devil	17
Southern Marsupial Mole	18
Numbat	19
Greater Bilby	20
Southern Brown Bandicoot	21
Koala	22
Common Wombat	23
Southern Hairy-nosed Wombat	24
Common Brushtail Possum	25
Spotted Cuscus	26
Common Ringtail Possum	27
Eastern Pygmy-possum	28
Leadbeater's Possum	29
Greater Glider	30
Sugar Glider	31
Feathertail Glider	32
Striped Possum	33

Honey Possum	34
Musky Rat-kangaroo	35
Long-nosed Potoroo	36
Red-legged Pademelon	37
Quokka	38
Swamp Wallaby	39
Yellow-footed Rock-wallaby	40
Red-necked (Bennett's) Wallaby	41
Whiptail Wallaby	42
Bridled Nailtail Wallaby	43
Lumholtz's Tree-kangaroo	44
Eastern Grey Kangaroo	45
Red Kangaroo	46
Common Wallaroo (Euro)	47
Spectacled Flying-fox	48
Grey-headed Flying-fox	49
Ghost Bat	50
Large-footed Myotis	51
Bush Rat	52
Water Rat	53
Spinifex Hopping-mouse	54
Western Pebble-mound Mouse	55
Leopard Seal	56
Australian Sea-lion	57
Dugong	58
Bottlenose Dolphin	59
Humpback Whale	60
Dingo	61
Glossary	62
Recommended further reading	63
Index and checklist	64

Australia's mammals

A mammal is a warm-blooded, furry animal that feeds its young on milk. This field guide describes some of Australia's **native** mammals, such as kangaroos, possums, bandicoots and bats.

Introduced mammals were imported after 1788. Some, such as goats, pigs and rabbits, have run wild and compete with native mammals for food, shelter and water. Others, such as foxes and cats, eat native mammals.

Where to start?

Many Australian mammals are shy or rare, and most are active at night. Introduced mammals are often easier to spot in the wild. However, possums, bandicoots, flying-foxes, insectivorous bats, native rodents and antechinus may visit suburban backyards. Kangaroos and wallabies may lose their fear of humans where they are protected, such as in national parks. Seals, whales and dolphins can be seen at the coast.

How to see mammals

- Go to a zoo and visit the walk-through and nocturnal exhibits.
- Go to a national park or wildlife sanctuary.
- Walk through the bush. Look up in trees and under bushes.
- Sit quietly by a creek. Search for mammal tracks and droppings.
- Walk, ride a bicycle or travel by car along outer suburban roads at dawn.
- Go on a trip to watch whales, seals or flying-foxes.
- Watch for dolphins and whales at the beach.
- Make contact with people who care for injured native animals (ask your State wildlife body for details).
- Watch for bats flying out from their roosts at dusk.
- Wherever you go, stay on full alert for flashes of fur.
- Never try to handle or feed wild animals!

When watching...

Make like a tree. Mammals have keen senses. When startled, they freeze, and then escape. If you try to make yourself into part of the landscape, the animals will know you are there, but with luck they may ignore you.

Some hints

- Wear clothes that don't rustle or flap.
- Move slowly and smoothly.
- Approach in a zigzag.
- Stalk against the wind. Freeze when the animal looks at you.
- Keep moving when it relaxes.

Some don'ts

- Don't carry a stick or stone.
- Don't talk loudly, or move suddenly.
- Don't take your dog.
- Don't expect to see mammals at midday.
- Try dawn, dusk and clear nights.

What am I seeing?

Read books on animal behaviour to discover reasons why mammals act as they do.

What mammal is it?

To help identify a mammal, note:

Size – Relate size to well-known mammals, e.g. mouse, rat, cat, dog.
Shape – Note head, neck, body, tail, legs.
Colour – What colour is where? Name parts of the body as shown below.
Habitat – Where does the mammal feed and shelter? Is this natural or not?
Range – Is this mammal likely to be in this area?
Food – What is it eating?
Collect droppings – If available, take to a museum in a sealed plastic bag for identification.

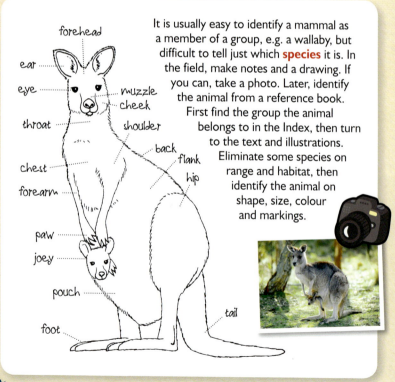

It is usually easy to identify a mammal as a member of a group, e.g. a wallaby, but difficult to tell just which **species** it is. In the field, make notes and a drawing. If you can, take a photo. Later, identify the animal from a reference book. First find the group the animal belongs to in the Index, then turn to the text and illustrations. Eliminate some species on range and habitat, then identify the animal on shape, size, colour and markings.

Naming mammals

A mammal is given:

1. An official common name
e.g. Common Wombat.

2. A scientific name
e.g. *Vombatus ursinus*. This is used all over the world. It is written in italics, and the word order is reversed from the order used in English. In this Guide the scientific name is followed by a translation (*Vombatus ursinus* means 'bear-like wombat').

3. Unofficial local names
e.g. Naked-nosed Wombat, Forest Wombat.

Abbreviations used in this book

HB = length of head + body
T = length of tail
HBT = length of head + body + tail
W = weight
♀ = female ♂ = male
Aust. = mainland Australia
Tas. = Tasmania only
NSW = New South Wales
WA = Western Australia
Qld = Queensland
Vic. = Victoria
SA = South Australia
NT = Northern Territory
Note: Where there is a great size difference between female and male of one species, average measurements for each sex are given.
Words in Red = Glossary

Spot the mammal

There are three groups of mammals in Australia.

1. Monotremes
Whose babies hatch from eggs, e.g. echidna.

(Short-beaked Echidna, a monotreme)

2. Marsupials
Whose newborn babies attach to their mothers' nipples to complete developing (usually in a pouch), e.g. wallaby.

(Red-necked Wallabies are marsupials)

3. Placental Mammals
Whose babies are born well-developed, e.g. bat.

(Grey-headed Flying-fox, a placental mammal)

Nearly 20 species of Australian mammals have become **extinct** in the past 200 years. At present, another 22 species are considered to be in danger of extinction.

Left: The Thylacine is now extinct

Monotreme, marsupial or placental mammal?

MONOTREMES

Platypus	10	Echidna	11

MARSUPIALS

Phascogale	12	Sugar Glider	31
Dunnart	14	Feathertail Glider	32
Quoll	16	Striped Possum	33
Tasmanian Devil	17	Honey Possum	34
Marsupial Mole	18	Musky Rat-kangaroo	35
Numbat	19	Long-nosed Potoroo	36
Greater Bilby	20	Pademelon	37
Bandicoot	21	Quokka	38
Koala	22	Swamp Wallaby	39
Common Wombat	23	Rock-wallaby	40
Southern Hairy-Nosed Wombat	24	Red-necked Wallaby	41
Brushtail Possum	25	Whiptail Wallaby	42
Spotted Cuscus	26	Bridled Nailtail Wallaby	43
Common Ringtail Possum	27	Tree-kangaroo	44
Pygmy-possum	28	Grey Kangaroo	45
Leadbeater's Possum	29	Red Kangaroo	46
Greater Glider	30	Common Wallaroo	47

PLACENTAL MAMMALS

Antechinus	13	Hopping-mouse	54
Kultarr	15	Western Pebble-mound Mouse	55
Spectacled Flying-fox	48	Leopard Seal	56
Grey-headed Flying Fox	49	Sea-lion	57
Ghost Bat	50	Dugong	58
Myotis	51	Dolphin	59
Bush-rat	52	Whale	60
Water Rat	53	Dingo	61

Platypus
Ornithorhynchus anatinus (= duck-like bird-bill)

Length:
HBT ♀ 37–55
♂ 40–63 cm

Weight:
♀ 600–1700
♂ 800–3000 g

Identification: Cat-sized freshwater mammal with smooth brown fur. Has leathery bill, no external ears, flattened body, broad tail and webbed feet. Makes a V-shaped bow-wave when swimming.

Where found: In or near fresh water along east coast Aust. and Tas.

Habits: Active at dawn and dusk. Catches small animals underwater, stores them in cheek pouches and surfaces to eat. Digs rest burrows in riverbank. Female lays two rubbery eggs, 17 mm in diameter, which **incubate** for 2 weeks in nest burrow. Feeds young on milk from patches on her belly for 4–5 months.

Notes: Male can inject **venom** through spurs on ankles. Baby has milk teeth, but loses them at **weaning**.

Status: Common but disappears when habitat altered.

Similar species: Water Rat has visible ears, thin tail and 'dogpaddles' when swimming.

Habitat: Creeks & Rivers

Food: Water Animals

Short-beaked Echidna
Tachyglossus aculeatus (= spiny fast-tongue)

Length: HB 30–45 cm

Weight: 2–7 kg

Identification: Cat-sized, spine-covered, long-snouted ground animal, with powerful claws and small tail.

Where found: All over Aust. and Tas.

Habits: Active at night and on dull winter days. Claws into ant and termite nests, pulls out insects with sticky tongue. Female lays one egg, incubates it for 10 days in her pouch, and suckles young for 12 weeks (in pouch, then in burrow).

Notes: Male has spurs, but no venom. Digs into ground or wedges into hollow when threatened. 'Trains' of several males follow one female in early spring, hoping to mate with her. Droppings contain soil.

Status: Common. Secure.

Similar species: None.

Habitat: Most Habitats

Food: Ants & Termites

Brush-tailed Phascogale

Phascogale tapoatafa (= pouched-weasel called by Aborigines tapoatafa)

Length: HB 15–26 cm; T 16–23 cm

Weight: 110–310 g

Identification: Rat-sized tree-dweller with soft grey body fur, pointed snout and very bushy black tail. Runs up and down trunks, on and under branches, and can leap 2 m between trees.

Where found: Open coastal forests around Aust.

Habits: Spends day in tree hollow, at night hunts insects and small animals; also eats nectar. Female carries 3–8 young on nipples for 7 weeks, then feeds them in nest for 13 weeks.

Notes: Fast and agile. Prefers rough-barked trees. Can rotate hindfoot 180° to climb up or down. When alarmed, taps forefeet on branch. All males die after mating (from stress-related illnesses). Females survive to give birth.

Status: Near threatened. Habitat destruction, cats, foxes.

Similar species: Rare Red-tailed Phascogale has upper part of tail rust-red.

Habitat: Coastal Forests

Food: Insects & Small Animals

Yellow-footed Antechinus

Antechinus flavipes (= yellow-footed hedgehog-like* animal)

Length: HB 9–16 cm; T 7–15 cm

Weight: 20–80 g

Identification: Looks like large mouse; big ears and eyes, and longish pointed snout. Grey head, light rings around eyes; reddish rump, belly and sides; yellow-brown feet. Black tail tip.

Where found: Many habitats, including gardens. Coastal eastern Aust. and south-western WA.

Habits: Spends day in nest under log or leaves. At night hunts insects and small animals. Moves in quick rushes, searches leaf litter, and climbs.

Notes: May enter houses looking for mice and spiders. In spring, males mate for up to 12 hours straight then die. Females carry up to 12 young for 5 weeks, and wean them at around 3 months.

Status: Common. Secure. Often caught by cats.

Similar species: Brown Antechinus is grey-brown above, lacks light eye-rings.

* Damp antechinus fur looks spiky.

Habitat: Coastal Habitats

Food: Insects & Small Animals

Fat-tailed Dunnart

Sminthopsis crassicaudata (= fat-tailed mouse-like animal)

Length: HB 6–9 cm; T 4–7cm

Weight: 10–20 g

Identification: Large-mouse-sized, grey-brown hunter with large ears and fat tail. Large eyes, dark eye-rings, pointed muzzle; long, narrow hindfeet.

Where found: Woodlands, grasslands, plains, farmlands, across southern and central Aust.

Habits: Shelters during day in nest hole, or under log. Hunts at night for insects and small animals. Usually 5 young, carried in well-developed pouch for 5 weeks, fed in nest for 5 weeks.

Notes: Several may share nest in cold weather. Does not need to drink water. Fat in tail is winter food reserve. May have increased range with clearing of land.

Status: Common. Secure.

Similar species: Stripe-faced Dunnart is a fat-tailed, inland species with dark facial stripe.

Habitat: Woodlands & Plains

Food: Insects & Small Animals

Kultarr

Antechinomys laniger (= woolly-furred mouse-like animal)

Length: HB 7–10 cm; T 10–15 cm

Weight: 20–30 g

Identification: Large-mouse-sized hunter with long hindlegs; long, tufted tail. Brown-grey back, white belly. Very large ears; large, bulging eyes.

Where found: Desert, inland plains, stony and sandy habitats.

Habits: Shelters during day in logs, clay cracks or under bushes. Hunts at night for insects, spiders and small animals. Female carries 6–8 young, protected by fold of skin on belly, for 4 weeks, then left in nest. Later ride on mother's back while she hunts.

Notes: An active desert predator. Bounds rather than hops.

Status: Probably secure. Vulnerable to habitat changes.

Similar species: None.

Habitat: Inland Desert

Food: Insects & Small Animals

Spotted-tailed Quoll

Dasyurus maculatus (= spotted hairy-tailed animal)

Length: HB ♀ 31–45 ♂ 33–76 cm; T ♀ 30–42 ♂ 31–55 cm

Weight: ♀ 0.8–2.5 ♂ 0.9–5 kg

Identification: Small-dog-sized **predator**. Brown fur with white spots; long spotted tail. Five toes on front and back feet. Bounds on ground, climbs trees. Makes a range of sounds, including hissing.

Where found: Isolated forests along east coast of Aust. and in Tas.

Habits: Prey ranges from insects to small wallabies, also **carrion**. Droppings made in special places in territory. Mating occurs in winter and lasts up to 17 hours. Female develops pouch, 5 young remain there for 7 weeks.

Notes: Largest marsupial predator on mainland.

Status: Threatened, declining. Habitat destruction, competition with fox and cat.

Similar species: No other quolls have spotted tails; Eastern Quoll rarely recorded on mainland.

Habitat: Forests & Woodlands

Food: Live Animals & Carrion

Tasmanian Devil

Sarcophilus harrisii (= Harris's flesh-lover)

Length: HB ♀ 57 ♂ 65 cm; T ♀ 24 ♂ 26 cm

Weight: ♀ 5–9 ♂ 8–14 kg

Identification: Black predator and scavenger with white markings on chest and rump. Looks like a medium-sized, bulky dog. Bounding **gait**. Makes a range of sounds: barking, growling and screaming.

Where found: Forests, woodlands and scrub in Tas.

Habits: Spends day in den or thick brush. Hunts from dusk to dawn for insects, small animals and carrion. Can climb trees. Female has 15–20 young in April, 4 survive to be carried in rear-opening pouch for 16 weeks, then left in den. Independent at 6–9 months.

Notes: Largest living marsupial **carnivore**. Lived on mainland until around 400 years ago. Group feeding at carcass may squabble loudly.

Status: Endangered, declining. Disease, competition from foxes.

Similar species: None.

Habitat: All over Tasmania

Food: Live Animals & Carrion

Southern Marsupial Mole

Notoryctes typhlops (= blind southern digger)

Length: HB 7–11 cm; T 1.5–2.5 cm

Weight: 40–70 g

Identification: Rat-sized burrowing marsupial with golden silky fur; blind, horny shield on nose, no visible ears. Two bladelike front claws are used for digging and gripping prey.

Where found: Sandy deserts of central Aust.

Habits: The Marsupial Mole lives in sand, digging tunnels that collapse behind it. Rarely surfaces. Eats insects, spiders and small reptiles found underground. Female has rear-opening pouch and two nipples.

Notes: Little known. Adapted to life underground, the Marsupial Mole looks very like the true moles, which are unrelated placental mammals.

Status: Endangered. It is very rarely seen.

Similar species: Northern Marsupial Mole is slightly smaller and only found in WA.

Habitat: Sandy Deserts

Food: Burrowing Animals

Numbat

Myrmecobius fasciatus (= banded ant-eater)

Length: HB 20–29 cm; T 12–21 cm

Weight: 305–750 g

Identification: Cat-sized marsupial. Red-brown fur on back with dark rump and white stripes; pale belly. Narrow head, sharp muzzle, dark stripe through eye. Long tail 'bottle-brushes' when active.

Where found: Survives in a few isolated eucalypt forests in South-West WA. Also re-introduced to 6 other sites where previously found.

Habits: Active during day. Shelters and sleeps in a hollow fallen log or burrow. Feeds on termites, scratched and licked with long, slender tongue from under rotting wood or surface tunnels.

Notes: Once found across southern Aust. from western NSW to coast of WA. Four young born in January, carried for 5 months, then fed in nest for 5 months.

Status: Endangered, declining. Threatened by habitat loss, foxes, fires.

Similar species: None.

Habitat: Eucalypt Forests

Food: Termites

Greater Bilby

Macrotis lagotis (= hare-eared long-ear)

Length: HB 30–39 cm; T 20–29 cm

Weight: 800–2500 g

Identification: Small-cat-sized burrowing marsupial with very long, rabbit-like ears. Long pointed muzzle; soft, silky grey fur. Long black tail with white tip.

Where found: Desert areas of central Aust. with little free surface water.

Habits: Shelters during day in a burrow that may be 3 m long and nearly 2 m deep. Gets moisture from food: insects, seeds, fruits and **fungi**. Digs feeding holes 10–25 cm deep. Droppings may contain sand.

Notes: Once found in dry areas across southern Aust. Two young stay in the rear-opening pouch for about 11 weeks, then are left in burrow.

Status: Vulnerable, declining. Threatened by grazing, fire, rabbits, cats and foxes.

Similar species: The Lesser Bilby is much smaller. It is almost certainly **extinct**.

Habitat: Sandy Deserts

Food: Insects, Fruits & Seeds

Southern Brown Bandicoot

Isoodon obesulus (= rather fat equal-toothed* animal)

Length: HB 28–36 cm; T 9–14 cm

Weight: 400–1850 g

Identification: Small-cat-sized, ground-living marsupial with pointed muzzle, humped back and short, thin tail. Grey-brown fur with black bristle hairs above, paler below. Bounds and gallops when moving fast.

Where found: Coastal south-western and south-eastern Aust. and Tas. Areas with sandy soil and dense ground cover.

Habits: Solitary, active both day and night. Feeds on insects, earthworms and fungi, leaving conical holes in ground. Up to 6 young are carried in a rear-opening pouch; weaned at around 9 weeks.

Notes: Needs home range of up to 7 ha. to supply food needs. Individuals' ranges may overlap if food plentiful.

Status: Vulnerable, declining.

Similar species: The Long-nosed Bandicoot, found in eastern part of range, has longer pointed muzzle, larger ears and white feet.

* Refers to the length of the incisor teeth.

Habitat: Forests & Heaths

Food: Small Life & Fungi

Koala

Phascolarctos cinereus (= ash-coloured pouched bear)

Where found: In remaining eucalypt forest in eastern Aust.

Habits: Solitary, active at dusk and dawn. Well-camouflaged, usually seen high up in eucalypt trees. The low energy content of its diet means a Koala sleeps up to 20 hours per day. Female carries 1 young in rear-opening pouch for 6 months, then on her back for another 6 months.

Length: HB 65–82 cm

Weight: 4–15 kg

Identification: Medium-dog-sized, tree-dwelling marsupial with woolly grey or brown fur. Round belly, round face, circular furry ears, large and squarish black nose, and strong limbs with long, sharp claws. No visible tail.

Notes: Southern Koalas are larger than northern ones. Hunted for fur trade until 1927. **Vulnerable** to dogs when changing trees. Also threatened by habitat destruction, disease, car strike and bushfires.

Status: Vulnerable, declining.

Similar species: None.

Habitat: Eucalypt Forests

Food: Eucalyptus Leaves

Common Wombat

Vombatus ursinus (= bear-like wombat)

Length: HB 84–115 cm; T 2.5 cm

Weight: 22–39 kg

Identification: Burrower. Stocky build, size of a large dog. Large head, naked nose and short ears. Grey to brown, coarse fur, tiny tail.

Where found: Coastal ranges, forest, scrub and woodland from north-eastern NSW to south-eastern SA and Tas.

Habits: Solitary, night-active, several burrows are dug in an area. Eats native grasses, shrubs, roots. In winter, may **bask** or feed in daytime. Female carries 1 young in rear-opening pouch for 6–10 months; it follows her for another 11 months.

Notes: Not protected in parts of Victoria. Large, rectangular droppings are left on logs and rocks. Burrows may be up to 20 m long, with several chambers and entrances.

Status: Common, declining.

Similar species: Two Hairy-nosed Wombat species are rare with soft, silky fur and hairy noses.

Habitat: Forests & Woodlands

Food: Grasses & Shrubs

Southern Hairy-nosed Wombat

Lasiorhinus latifrons (= broad-headed hairy-nose)

Length: HB 84–111 cm; T 3–6 cm

Weight: 18–36 kg

Identification: Short legs; stocky head and body. Soft, silky grey or brown fur. Fine hair on nose. Pointed ears.

Where found: Woodland, shrubland and heath of southern Australia.

Habits: Active at night. Can live in harsh environments. Feeds alone on native grasses; sometimes shares burrows. One young born in spring stays in pouch for 6 months and leaves its mother at 12 months.

Notes: Smallest of the 3 wombats. Sometimes has white hair on nose and chest. Uses between 1 and 10 burrows. Excellent hearing and sense of smell. Can run faster than 40 km/hr over short distances.

Status: Common. Range is decreasing.

Similar species: The Northern Hairy-nosed Wombat is endangered and only found in Queensland.

Habitat: Woodlands & Shrublands

Food: Native Grasses

Common Brushtail Possum

Trichosurus vulpecula (= little fox-like hairy-tail)

Length: HB 35–55 cm; T 25–40 cm

Weight: 1.2–2.5 kg

Identification: Cat-sized possum with fox-like face and long oval ears. Grey fur on back, cream below. Black bushy tail has short naked area underneath. Agile climber; sits upright and holds food in its paws. Makes variety of sounds: coughs, hisses and screeches.

Where found: All over Aust., most habitats.

Habits: Spends day in hollow tree, cave or roof of building. At night eats leaves, flowers and fruits. Male marks territory with chin, chest and **anal** glands. Female carries 1 young for 4–5 months in pouch, then 2 months on back.

Notes: Once hunted for fur. Short-haired, copper form in Qld.; larger, woolly, dark grey form in Tas.

Status: Common. Range is decreasing.

Similar species: Mountain Brushtail Possum is larger with darker coat, short rounded ears and long naked area under tail.

Habitat: Most Habitats

Food: Leaves, Fruits & Flowers

Spotted Cuscus

Spilocuscus maculatus (= spotted spotted-cuscus)

Length: HB 35–58 cm; T 31–43 cm

Weight: 1.5–5 kg

Identification: Large, slow moving, cat-sized tree-dweller. Round, bare-skinned face may flush reddish; large eyes, tiny ears. **Prehensile** tail is ⅔ naked underneath. Thick, woolly fur. Male is blotched grey and white above; female is grey.

Where found: Rainforests of Cape York Peninsula, north of Coen, Qld.

Habits: Solitary. Spends day sleeping on branch or in leaves of forest canopy. At night, eats leaves, fruits and flowers. Large **canine** teeth suggest some animal food. Males are aggressive towards each other. Usually 1 young, carried in mother's pouch, then on her back.

Notes: Can travel across bare ground to reach rainforest fragments. May make sleeping platform of leaves and twigs.

Status: Near threatened. Needs suitable habitat for survival.

Similar species: Southern Common Cuscus is more possum-like with longer snout, larger ears and stripe on back.

Habitat: Nth Qld Rainforests

Food: Leaves & Flowers

Common Ringtail Possum

Pseudocheirus peregrinus (= wandering false-hand*)

Length: HB 30–35 cm; T 30–35 cm

Weight: 700–900 g

Identification: Small-cat-sized possum. White patch of fur behind each short ear. Long, prehensile, white-tipped tail, with naked area beneath. Colour varies from reddish brown to grey above, cream below. Makes a soft, high-pitched, twittering call.

Where found: Various treed habitats down east coast from Cape York Qld to Tas.

Habits: Spends day in a ball-shaped, leaf-lined nest in tree hollow or dense foliage. At night eats leaves and flowers. Pairs stay together for breeding season. Both parents care for the 2 young; carried in the female's pouch for 4 months, then left in nest or carried on back for 2 months.

Notes: Can digest eucalypt leaves; fond of rosebuds. Soft droppings produced in nest during day are eaten to extract extra nourishment.

Status: Common.

Similar species: Western Ringtail Possum, found only in South-West WA, is vulnerable.

* The tail serves as another hand.

Habitat: Forests & Towns

Food: Leaves & Flowers

Eastern Pygmy-possum

Cercartetus nanus (= dwarf cercartetus*)

Length: HB 7–11 cm; T 7.5–10.5 cm

Weight: 15–43 g

Identification: Mouse-sized possum with fat-based, prehensile tail and large ears. Fawn above, white below.

Where found: Down eastern coast from southern Qld to eastern SA, including Tas., in rainforest, eucalypts and heaths.

Habits: Solitary. Spends day in tree hollow or makes 6 cm spherical nest. At night eats pollen, nectar (gathered with brush-tipped tongue) and insects. Female carries 4 young in pouch for 4 weeks, then feeds them in nest for 5 weeks.

Notes: Becomes **torpid** in cold weather, using up fat stored in the base of the tail.

Status: Common. Seldom seen. Vulnerable in NSW and SA.

Similar species: Little Pygmy-possum, mainly in Tas., is smaller, with grey belly. Western Pygmy-possum found in southern SA and south-western WA.

* The meaning of this is unknown.

Habitat: Forests & Heaths

Food: Nectar, Pollen & Insects

Leadbeater's Possum

Gymnobelideus leadbeateri (= Leadbeater's naked* glider)

Length: HB 15–17 cm; T 14.5–18 cm

Weight: 100–135 (spring); 110–166 (autumn) g

Identification: Shy, rat-sized possum. Grey to brown above, with dark stripe from face down back; cream below. Long tail broadens to club shape at tip. Active leaper.

Where found: Only in mountain forests of Vic.'s central highlands.

Habits: Active at night. Colonies of 2–12, consisting of a breeding pair and offspring, nest together in a tree hollow. Feeds on insects, spiders found beneath bark and tree sap. Female carries 1–2 young in pouch for 3 months, then left in nest until 4 months of age.

Notes: Group membership signalled by scent. Group defends territory up to 2 ha. Species was not sighted 1909–1961.

Status: Endangered, declining. 70% of habitat is in timber-production forests, 30% is in nature reserves. Suitable nest holes are only found in trees over 190 years old.

Similar species: Sugar Glider has gliding **membranes**, and its tail does not broaden.

* Refers to lack of gliding membranes.

Habitat: Mountain Forests

Food: Insects & Tree Sap

Greater Glider

Petauroides volans (= flying Petaurus-like animal)

Length: HB 35–46 cm; T 45–60 cm

Weight: 900–1700 g

Identification: Rabbit-sized glider with large ears and long, fluffy coat. Short snout; long, furry tail. Dark-grey and cream colouring. Gliding membrane only stretches to front elbow.

Where found: Eucalypt forests of eastern Qld, NSW and Vic.

Habits: Silent. Active at night, spends day in tree hollow and feeds high up in trees. Females have 2 teats but bear only 1 young; carried in pouch until 3–4 months and independent at 9 months.

Notes: Can glide up to 100 m between trees. Glides with elbows bent and paws under chin. Tail is not prehensile.

Status: Endangered in some states, declining.

Similar species: Larger and fluffier than other gliders; very large ears. Gliding membrane stretches to front wrist or finger in other gliders.

Habitat: Eucalypt Forests

Food: Eucalypt Leaves

Sugar Glider

Petaurus breviceps (= short-headed rope-dancer)

Length: HB 16–21 cm; T 16.5–21 cm

Weight: ♀ 95–135 ♂ 115–160 g

Identification: Rat-sized glider; grey above, cream below. Dark stripe from forehead to middle of back. Membranes stretching from fifth fingers to first toes are used to glide up to 50 m between trees.

Where found: Coastal forests and woodland from Kimberley, WA, around to south-eastern SA and Tas.

Habits: Active at night. Colonies of up to 7 adults and their young live in tree hollows. Feeds on tree sap, nectar, pollen and insects. Female carries 2 young in pouch for 2–3 months, then left in nest until 4 months.

Notes: Group recognises members by scent. In cold weather, group huddles and may become torpid. May live in garden nest boxes.

Status: Common in suitable habitat.

Similar species: Leadbeater's Possum lives in limited habitat and lacks membranes. Squirrel Glider is larger with more pointed face and fluffier tail.

 Habitat: Coastal Forests **Food:** Sap, Nectar & Insects

Feathertail Glider

Acrobates pygmaeus (= pygmy acrobat)

Length: HB 6.5–8 cm; T 7–8 cm

Weight: 10–15 g

Identification: Fast moving, mouse-sized glider. Grey above, white below. Long tail has fringe of hair on either side giving it a feather-like appearance. Large, forward-facing eyes. Gliding membranes between elbows and knees.

Where found: Forests and woodlands of eastern Aust.

Habits: Active at night. Feeds on nectar with brush-tipped tongue; also eats pollen and insects. Groups of 3–5 feed and nest together in tree hollows or nests. Female carries 3–4 young in pouch for 9 weeks, fed in nest for 5 weeks. Female may carry reserve **embryos**, which develop after larger young are weaned.

Notes: World's smallest gliding mammal. Glides up to 28 m. Pads under toes, sharp claws and prehensile tail aid climbing.

Status: Common. Secure. Endangered in SA.

Similar species: None.

 Habitat: Forests & Woodlands

 Food: Nectar, Pollen & Insects

Striped Possum

Dactylopsila trivirgata (= three-striped naked-finger)

Length: HB 26 cm; T 33 cm

Weight: ♀ 310–475
♂ 430–545 g

Identification: Large-rat-sized, slender, black and white striped possum. Black ears, large front teeth and long, slender fourth finger. It has a strong, sweet odour.

Where found: Rainforests and woodlands from Iron Range, south to Townsville, Qld.

Habits: Active at night. A fast, agile climber, which leaps boldly between trees. Uses its sharp teeth to pull away bark, then pokes grubs or other insects out with its tongue, or hooks them out with its long fourth finger. Occasionally eats fruit and tree sap. Sleeps during day in tree hollow. Breeds year round; female has 2 young.

Notes: Noisy when fighting or mating; shrieking and gurgling.

Status: Common, declining. Limited habitat needs protection.

Similar species: No other tree-dwelling mammal has bold stripes.

Habitat: Rainforests Nth Qld

Food: Insects & Small Life

Honey Possum

Tarsipes rostratus (= long-nosed tarsier*-foot)

Length: HB 6.5–9 cm; T 7–10 cm

Weight: 7–16 g

Identification: Large-mouse-sized, long-snouted marsupial. Grey-brown above, with darker stripe down back; cream below. Long prehensile tail, eyes on top of head. Fingers and toes have broad tips and nails, not claws.

Where found: Coastal heaths of South-West WA.

Habits: Sleeps during the day in an old bird nest or hollow grasstree stem. Feeds on nectar and pollen, using long, brush-tipped tongue. Becomes torpid in cold weather. Female carries 2–3 young in pouch for 2 months, fed in nest for 2 weeks. Female may carry reserve embryos, which develop after young are weaned.

Notes: Has fewer teeth than other marsupials. Depends on a variety of banksias, grevilleas, etc. for food. Acts as pollinator.

Status: Common. Secure.

Similar species: The Western Pygmy-possum has a much shorter muzzle; shorter, fatter tail; larger ears and softer fur.

* Tarsiers, like humans, have nails rather than claws

Habitat: Coastal Heaths, WA

Food: Nectar & Pollen

Musky Rat-kangaroo

Hypsiprymnodon moschatus (= musky* animal with teeth like a potoroo)

Length: HB 15–27 cm; T 12–16 cm

Weight: 360–680 g

Identification: Large-rat-sized **macropod** with long, scaly tail. Grey head, brown body. The smallest kangaroo relative and the only one to have 5 toes on hindfoot. Moves in bounds.

Where found: Rainforests of North Qld, from Ingham to Cooktown.

Habits: Feeds during the day on fruits, seeds, nuts, fungi and insects. Sleeps at night in a nest on the forest floor. Two young are carried in the pouch for 5 months, then fed in nest.

Notes: Similar to possums in having a 'big toe' and simple stomach (so it cannot digest grass). It hides seeds in the leaf litter, then eats them later. Can lose up to ¼ of body weight when food is scarce.

Status: Common. Secure. Needs rainforest for survival.

Similar species: None.

* Musk is a strong animal scent.

Habitat: Rainforests

Food: Fruits, Insects & Fungi

Long-nosed Potoroo

Potorous tridactylus (= three-toed potoroo)

Length: HB ♀ 26–38 ♂ 29–41 cm; T ♀ 20–25 ♂ 20–26 cm

Weight: ♀ 660–1350 ♂ 740–1640 g

Identification: Cat-sized macropod, grey-brown or red-brown fur above, paler below. Feet shorter than head. Bare skin from nose and up long snout. May have white tail tip.

Where found: Coastal forests and heaths with thick ground cover and sandy soils in south-eastern Aust. and Tas.

Habits: Moves like a little kangaroo. Feeds from dusk, digging small holes for roots, fungi and insects. Also eats fruits and seeds. Stays in or near cover. One young, carried in pouch for 4 months.

Notes: One of the first mammals to be named in Australia. It has disappeared as its habitat has been cleared.

Status: Vulnerable, declining.

Similar species: Endangered Long-footed Potoroo, found in small areas in north-eastern Vic. and south-eastern NSW, is larger and has longer hindfeet.

Habitat: Forests & Heaths

Food: Fruits, Insects & Fungi

Red-legged Pademelon

Thylogale stigmatica (= pricked-pattern* pouched-weasel)

Length: HB 39–54 cm; T 30–47 cm

Weight: ♀ 2.5–4 ♂ 3.5–7 kg

Identification: Small-dog-sized, stocky macropod with short, thick tail and soft fur. Grey-brown above, cream below. Reddish cheeks, arms and hindlegs.

Where found: Coastal rainforests and wet eucalypt forests of eastern Aust., from Cape York, Qld, to Sydney, NSW.

Habits: Feeds on leaves, fallen fruits and seeds in forest during day, grasses on edges at night. Rarely grazes more than 70 m from forest edge, moving rapidly along runways.

Notes: Rests with tail forward under body. Warning alarm thump made with hindfeet. One **joey** is carried in pouch for 28 weeks, weaned 9 weeks later.

Status: Common, declining. Vulnerable in NSW.

Similar species: Red-necked Pademelon has reddish fur on neck, but not on hindlegs.

* Refers to faint dotted markings on neck and hip.

Habitat: Rainforests & Eucalypt Forests

Food: Leaves, Grasses & Fruits

Quokka

Setonix brachyurus (= bristle-footed short-tail)

Length: HB ♀ 39–50 ♂ 43–54 cm; T ♀ 23–28 ♂ 25–31 cm

Weight: ♀ 1.6–3.5 ♂ 2.7–4.2 kg

Identification: Large-cat-sized, solid build macropod. Greyish-brown, coarse fur. Short, round ears; short, stiff tail.

Where found: On Rottnest Is., off WA, and in wetter parts of South-West WA.

Habits: Feeds on grass, leaves and stems; gathers near fresh water. One joey stays in the pouch about 6 months. Females may carry an embryo, which continues development after the joey is weaned.

Notes: Once common on south-western mainland. The second Australian marsupial to be named in 1696. Originally thought to be a big rat.

Status: Vulnerable, decreasing. Rarely seen on mainland.

Similar species: On mainland, rare Brush-tailed Bettong is larger and yellowish grey. It has a longer tail with a black crest of hair.

 Habitat: Forests & Heaths

 Food: Leaves & Herbs

Swamp Wallaby

Wallabia bicolor (= two-coloured wallaby)

Dark face with light brown cheek stripe. Black paws and tail-tip.

Where found: Forests, woodlands and heaths of eastern and southern Aust.

Habits: Shelters in dense undergrowth. Mainly solitary, sometimes feeds in groups. Breeds all year. One joey is born, leaves pouch at 9 months and is weaned at 15 months.

Notes: Hops differently to other wallabies with head low and tail straight out behind. Sometimes called a 'Stinker'.

Length: HB ♀ 66–75 ♂ 72–85 cm; T ♀ 64–73 ♂ 69–86 cm

Weight: ♀ 10–15 ♂ 12–20 kg

Identification: Medium-dog-sized wallaby with coarse fur. Dark brown to black on back and creamy yellow on belly.

Status: Common and widespread. Secure.

Similar species: Very dark colour distinguishes it from all other species of wallabies.

Habitat: Forests & Heaths

Food: Grasses & Shrubs

Yellow-footed Rock-wallaby

Petrogale xanthopus (= yellow-footed rock-weasel)

Length: HB 48–65 cm; T 57–70 cm

Weight: 6–11 kg

Identification: A colourful wallaby that hops across rocks. Grey-fawn above, white below; white stripe on cheek, side and hip. Ears, arms, hindlegs and feet are orange to yellow. Tail is ringed with orange and dark brown.

Where found: Dry, rocky country in Flinders Ranges, SA, and Adavale Basin, Qld.

Habits: Active at night during summer, during day and night in winter. Lives in colonies of up to 100. Eats grasses and leaves. One young in pouch for 6–7 months.

Notes: Has disappeared from much of former range since European settlement. Was previously hunted for its fur. Competes with feral goats and rabbits for food; preyed on by foxes, cats and eagles.

Status: Vulnerable.

Similar species: No other wallaby has coloured rings on its tail.

Habitat: Arid Rocky Country

Food: Grasses & Leaves

Red-necked (Bennett's*) Wallaby

Macropus rufogriseus (= red-grey long-foot)

Length: HB 65–92 cm; T 62–88 cm

Weight: 11–27 kg

Identification: Medium-sized wallaby; grey to reddish above, pale grey below. Distinct reddish-brown neck. Black muzzle, paws and largest toe. White stripe on upper lip.

Where found: Eucalypt forests of south-eastern Aust. and Tas. Grazes in open grassy areas bordering forest.

Habits: Solitary, but may feed in groups. Spends day resting in forest, grazing on grasses and leaves from late afternoon.

Notes: Group splits into single animals when disturbed. Protected in Aust. but may be killed under pest licence in Qld and Tas. Joey carried in pouch for 9–10 months, then suckled for another 4–5 months. Reserve embryo develops and is born after joey leaves pouch.

Status: Common. Secure.

Similar species: Black-striped Wallaby in Qld and northern NSW has dark stripe down back and white stripe on hip.

* Name of the species in Tasmania.

 Habitat: Eucalypt Forests

Food: Grasses & Leaves

Whiptail Wallaby

Macropus parryi (= Parry's long-foot)

Dark-brown forehead and base of ears; white stripe on upper lip. White stripe on hip and brown stripe down neck to shoulder.

Where found: Coastal forests of eastern Aust. from Cooktown, Qld, to northern NSW.

Habits: Feeds morning and afternoon on grasses, herbs and ferns; rests in hot middle of day. Lives in groups of up to 50; **dominant** male mates with female. Joey carried in pouch for 8–9 months, then suckled for another 4–7 months. Reserve embryo develops when pouch is vacant.

Length: HB ♀ 61–88 ♂ 74–100 cm; T ♀ 73–86 ♂ 86–105 cm

Weight: ♀ 7–15 ♂ 14–26 kg

Identification: Medium-sized wallaby; grey or brownish-grey above, white below. Long, slender tail with dark tip.

Notes: Also called Pretty-face Wallaby. When alarmed, thumps ground with hindfeet.

Status: Common. Secure.

Similar species: Black-striped Wallaby has dark back stripe.

Habitat: Forests & Woodlands

Food: Grasses & Herbs

Bridled Nailtail Wallaby

Onychogalea fraenata (= bridled nailed-weasel)

Length: HB ♀ 43–54 ♂ 51–70 cm; T ♀ 36–44 ♂ 38–54 cm

Weight: ♀ 4–6 ♂ 5–8 kg

Identification: Small wallaby with horny 'nail' at tip of tail. Grey-brown above; paler sides and belly. White 'bridle' stripe from back of neck to underarm. Dark stripe from nose to eye; pale cheek stripe to below eye. Long, slim ears.

Where found: Woodlands and shrublands; in three areas of central Qld and one area of south-western NSW.

Habits: Eats native grasses, soft ground plants and shrubs. Rests alone under thick bushes by day; feeds from dusk in small groups. Joey stays in pouch for 4 months; reserve embryo develops when pouch vacant.

Notes: Thought to be extinct for over 30 years until one was spotted by a fencing worker in 1973 after he read a magazine article about extinct animals.

Status: Endangered. Eaten by dogs and foxes; competition from rabbits, sheep, cattle.

Similar species: Northern Nailtail Wallaby, *Onychogalea unguifera*, across northern Aust. is sandy coloured without a dark facial stripe.

Habitat: Woodlands & Shrublands

Food: Native Grasses & Shrubs

Lumholtz's Tree-kangaroo

Dendrolagus lumholtzi (= Lumholtz's tree-hare)

Length: HB ♀ 42–68 ♂ 52–71 cm; T ♀ 47–74 ♂ 66–80 cm

Weight: ♀ 5.1–7.75 ♂ 5.4–10 kg

Identification: Medium-sized, tree-climbing kangaroo with long non-prehensile tail, and strong front and hind limbs. Brownish-black colour, with lighter fur on lower back. Pale brown band across forehead and down each side of face; dark tail tip.

Where found: Highland rainforest; limited area of north-eastern Qld.

Habits: Solitary. Sleeps crouched in tree tops by day. Eats leaves and fruits. Joey stays in pouch for 8–9 months.

Notes: Shy, well camouflaged, difficult to find in habitat. Freezes to avoid being seen. If alarmed, will leap between trees or up to 15 m to the ground. Tree-kangaroos are the only kangaroos able to walk rather than hop.

Status: Common. Secure. Listed as near threatened in Qld.

Similar species: Bennett's Tree-kangaroo lacks pale head markings.

Habitat: Highland Rainforests

Food: Leaves & Fruits

Eastern Grey Kangaroo

Macropus giganteus (= gigantic long-foot)

Length: HB ♀ 96–186 ♂ 97–230 cm; T ♀ 45–84 ♂ 43–110 cm

Weight: ♀ 17–42 ♂ 19–85 kg

Identification: Large grey or grey-brown kangaroo with paler underparts. Unlike other kangaroos, has hair on muzzle between nostrils and upper lip.

Where found: Forest, woodland, heathland, and scrubland; from inland plains to eastern coastal Aust. and north-eastern Tas.

Habits: Rests in the shade during day; eats grasses from late afternoon to early morning. Males are larger than females; dominant males mate with most females. Joey carried in pouch for 11 months, suckles for another 7 months. Reserve embryo develops when pouch vacant.

Notes: Numbers have increased using water and feed provided for cattle and sheep.

Status: Common. Secure.

Similar species: The Western Grey Kangaroo is browner than the Eastern Grey, and its range lies more to the west.

Habitat: Forests, Shrublands & Heathlands

Food: Grasses

Red Kangaroo

Macropus rufus (= red long-foot)

Length: HB ♀ 75–110 ♂ 94–140 cm; T ♀ 65–90 ♂ 71–100 cm

Weight: ♀ 17–39 ♂ 22–92 kg

Identification: Very large kangaroo. Males are red, females blue-grey or reddish above; white below. Black and white patches at sides of muzzle, white stripe from mouth to ear. Horizontal hop.

Where found: Inland plains and woodlands, with available water.

Habits: Rests during heat of day, feeds on grasses from dusk. Small groups are led by a dominant male. In drought, breeding activity slows and joeys die. After rain, when green feed is available, breeding is successful.

Notes: Adapted to hot, arid environment. Harvested under permits for meat and skins.

Status: Common. Secure. Has increased since European settlement.

Similar species: Wallaroos and grey kangaroos lack facial markings.

 Habitat: Inland Plains **Food:** Grasses

Common Wallaroo (Euro)

Macropus robustus (= robust long-foot)

Length: HBT ♀ 111–158 ♂ 114–199 cm

Weight: ♀ 6.3–28 ♂ 7.3–60 kg

Identification: Large, stocky macropod; dark brown or light grey above, paler below. Fur coarse and longer than other kangaroos. Area between nostril and lip is naked. Hops upright.

Where found: Various habitats with rocky hills. Most of Aust., except central north, south-west and south-east. Not in Tas.

Habits: Solitary. Shelters under ledges during day; eats mostly grasses, sometimes shrubs, at night. Can survive 3 months without water. One joey in pouch for 8–9 months. Reserve embryo develops when pouch vacant.

Notes: Large male may be twice female weight. Called different names in eastern and western Aust., e.g. Euro, Eastern Wallaroo, Red Wallaroo, Roan Wallaroo.

Status: Common. Secure.

Similar species: Antilopine Wallaroo, prefers flatter country in northern Aust.; has white fringing on ears and swollen black nose. Black Wallaroo in far central north Aust. is dark brown-black with shorter ears.

Habitat: Rocky Hill Slopes

Food: Grasses & Shrubs

Spectacled Flying-fox

Pteropus conspicillatus (= spectacled wing-foot)

Length: HB 22–24 cm

Weight: ♀ 450–800 g
♂ 500–1000 g

Identification: Large **megabat** with black body and wings. Yellowish fur around eyes and down muzzle; neck ruff of yellow hair. Male ruff may be reddish from scent marking fluid.

Where found: Camps and feeds in or near rainforest in north-eastern Qld.

Habits: Spends day in camp, flies out at dusk to feed on fruit. Can move large distances each night. One young nursed by mother for 3–5 months.

Notes: Feeds on rainforest fruits. Carries fruit away to eat, or passes seeds through gut, so helps rainforest regeneration and also pollination.

Status: Vulnerable. Disappears as rainforest is cleared.

Similar species: Other flying-foxes lack pale eye rings or 'spectacles'.

 Habitat: NE Qld Rainforest **Food:** Rainforest Fruits

Grey-headed Flying-fox

Pteropus poliocephalus (= grey-headed wing-foot)

Length: HB 23–29 cm

Weight: 300–1100 g

Identification: Very large megabat with thick grey fur and black wings. Reddish-yellow neck ruff. Fur on legs goes all the way to ankles.

Where found: Coastal forests and woodlands near watercourses, eastern Aust.

Habits: Spends day in camps and flies out to feed on blossoms and fruits at night. One young is carried for 4–5 weeks, then left and fed in colony until 12 weeks.

Notes: Important to forest; spreads seeds and pollen. Can fly faster than 60 km/hr and travel over 50 km in one night. Very vocal, has over 30 different calls.

Status: Vulnerable. Declining.

Similar species: In other flying-foxes, fur only goes down to knees. May interbreed with the Black Flying-fox.

Habitat: Forests & Woodlands

Food: Blossoms & Fruits

Ghost Bat
Macroderma gigas (= giant large-skin)

Length: HB 10–13 cm

Weight: 140–165 g

Identification: Large **microbat** with large eyes, large ears joined at their bases and a simple **noseleaf**. Fur grey above, paler below.

Where found: Scattered locations in diverse habitats across northern Aust. Roosts in caves, mine shafts, crevices.

Habits: Lives in colonies numbering from a few bats to over 400. At night swoops on small animals (frogs, lizards, birds, mammals and other bats). Holds prey in its wings, bites and kills them, then carries them to a perch to eat. One young born in spring.

Notes: Uses sight, sound and **echolocation** to navigate and find prey. Numbers have decreased in last 200 years mainly from habitat loss.

Status: Vulnerable. Decreasing.

Similar species: None.

Habitat: Roosts in Caves

Food: Small Animals

Large-footed Myotis

Myotis macropus (= large-footed mouse-ear)

Length: HB 5–5.5 cm; T 3.5–4 cm

Weight: 7–12 g

Identification: Mouse-sized microbat. Grey-brown or ginger above, paler below. Nose overhangs bottom lip; lacks noseleaf. Very large feet with flattened toes. Long tail.

Where found: Coastal forests of northern and eastern Aust. Always found near water.

Habits: Lives in colonies of 10–15 bats in caves, mines, tree hollows and buildings. One young born in spring or summer.

Notes: Becomes torpid in winter in southern states. Swoops over water to catch small fish, frogs and water insects in their feet. Also eats flying insects.

Status: Varies from common to endangered in different parts of range.

Similar species: Distinguished from other microbats by very large feet and flattened toes.

Habitat: Forests, Shrublands & Heathlands

Food: Grasses

Bush Rat
Rattus fuscipes (= dusky-footed rat)

Length: HB 11–21 cm; T 10–19 cm

Weight: 40–225 g

Identification: Rat with pink, rounded ears and soft, dense fur. Grey-brown or reddish-brown above, lighter below. Tail shorter than head and body.

Where found: Coastal forests, woodland and scrub with dense undergrowth in south-west, south-east and north-east Aust.

Habits: Active at night. Prefers thick undergrowth. Eats grass-stems and leaves, fruits, seeds, fungi and insects.

Notes: Five young born in a litter are independent of their mother at 4–5 weeks. Only the season's young survive winter to breed in springtime. In High Country of south-eastern NSW and north-eastern Vic.; lives in runways under snow in winter.

Status: Common. Secure. Sensitive to habitat change. Repopulates after rain.

Similar species: Introduced Black Rat has tail longer than body.

Habitat: Dense Undergrowth

Food: Grass, Seeds & Fungi

Water Rat

Hydromys chrysogaster (= golden-bellied water-rat)

Length: HB 23–37 cm; T 23–33 cm

Weight: ♀ 340–990 ♂ 400–1300 g

Identification: Large rat with dense fur. Grey to black above, white to orange below. Thick tail covered with hair and usually has a white tip. Blunt nose; small ears and eyes are high on head. Broad back feet are partly webbed.

Where found: Various habitats with fresh or brackish water. Northern, eastern and south-western Aust. and all of Tas.

Habits: Mainly active at sunset and night, sometimes during the day. Hunts mainly in water for insects, fish, yabbies, mussels and small animals. Also eats carrion and plants. Three or four young suckle for 4 weeks; leave mother at 8 weeks.

Notes: Food is carried to a feeding place where leftovers of past meals can be seen. Can travel large distances over land.

Status: Common. Secure.

Similar species: No other rat has partly webbed feet. Platypus has broad bill and tail.

Habitat: Creeks, Dams & Rivers

Food: Small Aquatic Life

Spinifex Hopping-mouse

Notomys alexis (= Alexandria Downs southern mouse)

Length: HB 9.5–11 cm; T 13–15 cm

Weight: 27–45 g

Identification: Light brown above, pale below. Large ears, long hindfeet and very long brush-tipped tail. Pouch under the throat with patch of bare skin.

Where found: Arid, sandy habitats in western and central Aust.

Habits: Shelters from heat of day in nest in deep burrow; active at night. Eats seeds, roots, flowers, fungi and insects.

Notes: Hopping mice use all four limbs when moving slowly; hop on hindfeet to move at speed. Three or four young left in nest while female looks for food. Either female or male retrieve young if they wander from nest.

Status: Common. Secure. Numbers fall in dry times and increase after rainfall.

Similar species: Short-tailed Hopping-mouse is probably extinct; Fawn Hopping-mouse in different habitat (gibber plains).

Habitat: Arid Sand Country

Food: Seeds, Fungi & Insects

Western Pebble-mound Mouse

Pseudomys chapmani (= Chapman's false-mouse)

Length: HB 5.2–6.7 cm; T 7.3–7.9 cm

Weight: 10–15 g

Identification: Pale brown above, with paler paws; white below. Long head, large ears. Tail longer than head and body.

Where found: Rocky grass and shrublands.

Now only in Pilbara area of WA. Old mounds suggest previously found in the Gascoyne and Murchison River areas as well.

Habits: Lives in burrows beneath mounds of stones or pebbles up to 10 g in weight. A mound may cover 0.5–9 m². Probably eats seeds and other vegetable material. Female bears several litters of 4 young each year.

Notes: First recorded in 1970s. Carries pebbles up to half its weight in mouth, then position them with forelimbs.

Status: Common and secure within limited habitat.

Similar species: None in same area.

Habitat: Stony Aridlands

Food: Seeds & Plants

Leopard Seal

Hydrurga leptonyx (= slender-clawed water-worker)

Length: HBT 300–360 cm

Weight: 400–600 kg

Identification: True seal with slim build, large head and distinct neck. Dark grey above, lighter below with spots on throat and sides. Jaws have wide gape. No ears.

Where found: Pack ice in southern oceans; southern Australian beaches and rocky shores.

Habits: Feeds on penguins, krill, fish, squid, other seals, seabirds and whale carcasses. The top of the southern ocean food chain. Female has 1 pup per breeding season, weaned at 4 weeks.

Notes: Solitary. Males and females sing to attract mates. Short front flippers cannot support body weight. When on land they inch along on their bellies.

Status: Common. Rare in SA.

Similar species: Fur seals have ears, lack spots and can sit upright on land.

 Habitat: Sea & Seashore

 Food: Marine Animals

Australian Sea-lion

Neophoca cinerea (= ash-coloured new-seal)

Length: HBT ♀ 130–185 ♂ 185–225 cm

Weight: ♀ 65–100 ♂ 180–250 kg

Identification: Eared seal with blunt snout and small rolled ears. On land, props itself upright on broad front flippers. Male dark with white crown and nape; female ash-grey above, cream below. Pups chocolate brown.

Where found: Offshore islands from the Abrolhos, WA, to Kangaroo Island, SA. Also some cliff bases on mainland.

Habits: Swims using front flippers. Feeds at sea on fish, squid and other marine creatures. Breeds on rocky or sandy beaches; one pup suckles up to 15 months of age.

Notes: Only seal or sea-lion found exclusively in Aust. Hunted to near-extinction by sealers; absent from Bass Strait. Aggressive while breeding.

Status: Endangered, decreasing.

Similar species: Australian Fur-seal has dense underfur.

Habitat: Sea & Seashore

Food: Fish, Squid & Shrimp

Dugong
Dugong dugon (= Dugong)

Length: HBT 315–331 cm

Weight: 420 kg

Identification: Large, round-bodied sea mammal with blunt muzzle and broad, bristled upper lip. Paddle-like front flippers; horizontal tail **flukes**. No dorsal fin. Grey to brown above, paler below.

Where found: In shallow, calm, warm coastal waters from Shark Bay, WA, around north of Aust. to Moreton Bay, Qld.

Habits: Lives in herds; feeds on seagrasses. Female breeds after 10–17 years of age. One calf rides just above her back and is weaned at 18 months.

Notes: Dense bones keep it on the bottom while using broad upper lip to direct seagrasses into the mouth.

Status: Vulnerable/endangered. Habitat damage, hunting, netting and boat accidents.

Similar species: Dolphins have pointed snouts and dorsal fins.

Habitat: Shallow Seas

Food: Seagrasses

Bottlenose Dolphin

Tursiops sp. (= porpoise-like animal)

Length: 240–380 cm

Weight: 180–500 kg

Identification: Streamlined marine mammal with short to medium-sized beak, rounded forehead and backward-pointing **dorsal** fin. Slender, pointed flippers. Blue-grey above, paler sides, white below.

Where found: Inshore or offshore waters anywhere around Aust. and Tas.

Habits: Usually in small groups. Often rides bow-waves of boats. Dives for up to 4 minutes, shows forehead but not beak when surfacing.

Notes: 2 Australian spp.: Indo-Pacific and Offshore Bottlenose Dolphin. Eats fish, squid and other marine animals. Inquisitive and active.

Status: Common. Probably secure.

Similar species: Other dolphins have different beak, head, and fin shapes; also different behaviour and colour patterns.

Habitat: Coasts & Seas

Food: Fish & Marine Life

Humpback Whale

Megaptera novaeangliae (= big-winged new-Englander)

Length: HBT up to 18 m

Weight: Up to 45 tonnes

Identification: Large whale with massive head. **Callosities** on top and on lower jaw; 14–35 grooves on throat. Flippers ⅓ as long as body; small dorsal fin. Blue-grey to black above, white below.

Where found: In winter, migrate from Antarctic waters up coasts of Australia to breed in warm sub-tropical waters then return in springtime.

Habits: Feeds on **krill**, filtered from Antarctic seas by **baleen** in mouth. Does not feed while migrating. Males compete for right to mate with females and also 'sing' by shifting air around spaces in their bodies.

Notes: All whales in an area sing the same song, which can change over time. Slow swimmer, dives for up to 45 minutes.

Status: Vulnerable. Numbers have been increasing since end of whaling.

Similar species: Southern Right Whale has blunt-ended flippers; large, lumpy white callosities on head.

Habitat: Seas

Food: Krill

Dingo
Canis lupus dingo (= dog-wolf)

Length: HB 81–111 cm; T 25–37 cm

Weight: 11–22 kg

Identification: Medium-sized dog, typically yellowish-ginger, sometimes black and tan or white. Usually white markings on chest, tail tip and paws. Pricked ears and bushy tail.

Where found: All Aust. except for Tas.

Habits: Lives in packs; breeds once a year. Only dominant male and female breed; others help rear pups. Takes any available prey from insects to large mammals such as kangaroos.

Notes: Developed from Indian Wolf around 6000 years ago; brought to Australia around 4000 years ago by seafarers. Considered by most to be a native animal because it has been here for so long.

Status: Vulnerable. At risk of being bred out by domestic dogs.

Similar species: Some breeds of domestic dog. Hybrids between Dingo and domestic dog are increasing.

Habitat: All Habitats

Food: Animals of all Sizes

Glossary

anal associated with final opening of digestive tract.
baleen in whales, fringed plates on upper jaw, used to strain sea water.
bask expose body to warmth.
callosities thick, hard skin areas.
canine pointed eye-tooth of mammal.
carnivore animal that kills and eats other animals.
carrion dead flesh.
dominant controlling.
dorsal on the back.
droppings digestive wastes; faeces.
echolocation use of high-pitched sounds to locate objects.
embryo animal or plant in early stages of its development.
extinct no longer in existence.
flukes flaps of a marine mammal's tail.
fungi group including moulds, yeasts and mushrooms.
gait way of moving.
habitat where an animal or plant lives.
incubates keeps at a constant temperature.
introduced brought from another place or country.
joey young of a macropod.
krill small crustaceans; shrimps.
macropod kangaroos, wallabies and their relatives.
megabat large fruit-eating bat.
membrane sheet-like connective tissue or thin, soft skin.
microbat small insect-eating bat.
native occurring naturally in that place or country.
noseleaf skin growth on muzzle of microbat, used in echo-location.
predator animal that kills to eat.
prehensile capable of grasping.
range geographical area in which an animal or plant occurs.
solitary living alone.
species group of similar animals that produces fertile offspring when mated.
status existing number of a species, and whether increasing or decreasing.
torpid state of reduced activity due to cold.
venom poison injected by an animal.
vulnerable exposed to injury.
weaning time of ceasing suckling.

Recommended further reading

Strahan, R. & Van Dyck, S. ed., 2008. *The Mammals of Australia*. Reed New Holland, Sydney.

Cronin, L., 2008. *Cronin's Key Guide to Australian Mammals*. Allen & Unwin, Sydney.

Queensland Museum and Parish, S., 2008. *Amazing Facts About Australian Mammals*. Pascal Press, Sydney.

Parish, S. and Cox, K., 2008. *Wild Australia Guide: Mammals*. Pascal Press, Sydney.

Parish, S. and Cox, K., 2008. *Wild Australia Guide: Sea Mammals*. Pascal Press, Sydney.

Parish, S. and Cox, K., 2008. *Wild Australia Guide: Kangaroos and Their Relatives*. Pascal Press, Sydney.

Parish, S. and Cox, K., 2008. *Wild Australia Guide: Bats*. Pascal Press, Sydney.

Lindsey, T. 1998. *Green Guide Mammals of Australia*. New Holland, Sydney.

Index and checklist ☑

- ☐ Antechinus, Yellow-footed 13
- ☐ Bandicoot, Southern Brown 21
- ☐ Bat, Ghost 50
- ☐ Bilby, Greater 20
- ☐ Cuscus, Spotted 26
- ☐ Devil, Tasmanian 17
- ☐ Dingo 61
- ☐ Dolphin, Bottlenose 59
- ☐ Dugong 58
- ☐ Dunnart, Fat-tailed 14
- ☐ Echidna, Short-beaked 11

Flying-fox
- ☐ Grey-headed 49
- ☐ Spectacled 48

Glider
- ☐ Feathertail 32
- ☐ Greater 30
- ☐ Sugar 31
- ☐ Hopping-mouse, Spinifex 54

Kangaroo
- ☐ Eastern Grey 45
- ☐ Red 46
- ☐ Koala 22
- ☐ Kultarr 15
- ☐ Mole, Southern Marsupial 18
- ☐ Mouse, Western Pebble-mound 55
- ☐ Myotis, Large-footed 51
- ☐ Numbat 19
- ☐ Pademelon, Red-legged 37

- ☐ Phascogale, Brush-tailed 12
- ☐ Platypus 10

Possum
- ☐ Common Brushtail 25
- ☐ Common Ringtail 27
- ☐ Honey 34
- ☐ Leadbeater's 29
- ☐ Striped 33
- ☐ Potoroo, Long-nosed 36
- ☐ Pygmy-possum, Eastern 28
- ☐ Quokka 38
- ☐ Quoll, Spotted-tailed 16

Rat
- ☐ Bush 52
- ☐ Water 53
- ☐ Rat-kangaroo, Musky 35
- ☐ Rock-wallaby, Yellow-footed 40
- ☐ Seal, Leopard 56
- ☐ Sea-lion, Australian 57
- ☐ Tree-kangaroo, Lumholtz's 44

Wallaby
- ☐ Bridled Nailtail 43
- ☐ Red-necked (Bennett's) 41
- ☐ Swamp 39
- ☐ Whiptail 42
- ☐ Wallaroo, Common (Euro) 47
- ☐ Whale, Humpback 60

Wombat
- ☐ Common 23
- ☐ Southern Hairy-nosed 24